Choosing the Correct Too

ɔ start making bead jewellery you will need a few simple suppli
lso need a well lit place to work and a little time to experiment v
ations. This book is a quick guide to identify the materials you
ɩw design ideas to stretch the supplies just that little bit further.

ɔols - You will need just a few basic hand tools:- round nosed pliers for making ɩɔɔ‿,
at faced pliers for gripping and squashing. Your flat faced pliers can be chain nosed (short and pointed
n the outside surface), snipe nosed (long and pointed) or flat nosed (blunt ended). You will also need
pair of scissors and a fleecy beadmat is useful for planning out your designs. If you are working with a
ɩe thread you will need a beading needle (see p.13).

Types of Beads

eads are available in a multitude of shapes, materials and sizes - you will also need to take into account
ɩeir weight; the size of the hole and the position of the hole when you make your design.

ɩlass beads - from tiny seed beads and Delicas to large handmade works of art these are the most com-
ɩonly available beads. Think about the weight of glass when you are making earrings and look out for
ɔugh edges on the holes if you need to use a fine beading thread.

ɩrystal - a higher lead content glass used for sparkling cut shapes and diamante.

Vooden Beads - easy to thread and available in non-toxic bright colours. Poke the holes with a knitting
ɩeedle to make the wood fibres lie flat and make threading easier.

ɩetal Beads - make sure they do not contain nickel. You will find them great for spacing larger beads and
ɔn't be afraid to mix different colours of metal in the same design.

emi-Precious Beads - stones shaped and drilled to be used for decoration - make sure that the hole is
ɩide enough all the way through the shape for your chosen threading material.

ɩastic Resin - Lucite, Perspex and Polythene can be moulded and coloured indefinitely - cheap plastic
eads can be horrid - make sure that you feel the weight and finish before you buy.

Hole Sizes and Positions Make a Difference to your Design

Through Hole	Top Hole	Cross Hole	Looped Beads	Large Central
The hole goes straight through the bead from side to side and it will hang centrally on your thread or wire. Most beads are of this type	Front to Back By threading this bead type straight onto a necklace you will just see the thin edge of the bead - it needs a ring or loop to turn it to face the front or to dangle as a charm or earring	Side to Side Will thread on and show well on a necklace or bracelet - needs a jump ring or loop to dangle properly for an earring or charm	Ready prepared to hang these just need a jump ring or a wire loop to link onto. Get the combination of loops and rings correct so the pendant dangles the right way around	Hole - Donut Needs a deco-rative thread or wire to attach to the rest of the design as the thread shows against the face side of the bead

To make a round loop you will need to use a pair of round nosed pliers. The noses on the pliers are cylindrical and taper to a point. Depending on where on the nose you wrap the wire you will get different sizes of loop (fig 1).

fig 1

To practice your loops use a headpin. Thread on a bead or beads and trim to leave 6 - 8mm showing at the top of the bead (fig 2). Using the tips of the pliers grip the pin immediately above the bead and tip back to 45° (fig 3).

Some larger beads will sit on the pin or wire more securely if you use a small bead or bead cup at each end

Making a Loop

Once you can make a loop you can make earrings, pendants, chains, tassels etc. If you have not made a loop before it is worthwhile practicing a little first - make five or ten practice loops and it will become much easier.

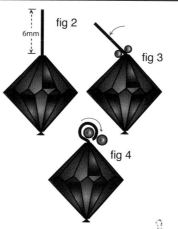

6mm

fig 2

fig 3

fig 4

You are aiming to make a centralised closed loop (fig 5) - if you need to make small adjustments use the very tips of the pliers.

fig 5

With your free hand grip the top bead. The bent pin end will swing around - bring the cut end to point at your chest. Grip the very end of the cut wire with your pliers 3mm from the tips of the tool nose. Roll the wrist of the hand holding the pliers away from yourself to form the loop (fig 4). Make sure that the loop has closed (fig 5).

Loop to Loop Linking

When you can make a loop you can start to link your beads into a longer dangle or a chain using eyepins

Bead a headpin dangle or first eyepin link to start the design. Complete this pin with a closed loop as above. Hold an eyepin vertically in front of you with the loop at the bottom. With your pliers grip the loop at 3 o'clock on the side of the loop that will open (nine o'clock if you are left handed) (fig 6).

Plain beads look more interesting whe separated out onto linked eyepins

fig 6

fig 7

With your index finger and thumb on your other hand grip the wire immediately above the loop. Roll your plier wris away from you to <u>twist</u> the loop open (fig 7) - do not pul the loop open. Pop in the prepared loop at the top of the headpin or first eyepin. Grip the open loop with the pliers in the same position as before and twist the loop shut. You are now ready to bead the wire above the link.

Simple Earrings & Loop to Loop Links

Small metallic beads top and bottom give a professional finish

Attaching a Fishhook Earwire

90°

Grip the front of the loop on the fishhook with the plier tips at 90° to the spring above the bead. Support the earwire by holding the bead and the spring firmly in your other hand. Rotate the pliers away from you just a tiny amount to twist the loop open. Do not twist too far or the loop will break - the wire on the loop has been put through a bending machine and is thus quite hard and can be brittle if you bend it too far.
Alternatively use a jump ring to bring several strands together onto the earwire loop.

Use metal spacers to separate similar beads

Three headpins trimmed to different lengths all hang from one eyepin loop

Small bead filigree cups help to support a larger bead on the end of a headpin

Try a small contrast bead on a separate link at the top of the design to elongate a stubby design

The loop does not have to be tight against the bead - leave a length of pin showing for an elegant earring style

Separate simple beads with loops for maximum impact and mobility when worn

Try Loops of Different Sizes

Use a piece of 0.6mm half hard wire or trim the small loop from the end of an eyepin to give you a short length of wire to work with. Make a loop using a thicker part of the round nosed pliers. This larger loop will be able to link more small loops together into a tassel or will pass through the cross-hole or top-hole of the bead you want to dangle from an earring or necklace.

The dangles on this necklace hang directly from the stranded beading wire - this makes them fan out around the neck profile.
If you use jump rings to connect the dangles to the threading wire they will be able to swing more freely and will tend to hang vertically

Making a Link with a Jump Ring

Jump rings are used for linking together components into chains and tassels and for attaching findings such as clasps, keyrings and earfittings. Many people struggle to open and close jump rings successfully but it is a simple technique that just requires a bit of practice - start with a larger jump ring and follow the directions below and you will soon 'get the knack'.

fig 8

fig 9

Jump rings must be opened and closed properly to maintain their shape and strength.

For right handers - With the gap in the jump ring at the top pointing to noon grip your first pair of pliers onto the jump ring at 3 o'clock. Use your other pair of pliers to come up from the 6 o'clock direction and grip the ring to cover 7 o'clock to 11 o'clock as fig 8. Hold the left hand pliers still and roll the right hand pair away from you to twist the ring open (fig 9). Pop onto the ring the components that you need to link together and place the pliers back on the ring as before. Roll the wrist back to close the ring.
For left handers - Reverse the diagram and hold the first pair at 9 o'clock and the second pair to cover 5 o'clock to 1 o'clock. Roll the left wrist to open and close the ring.

Pendant pieces with front to back holes need a jump ring before they can run onto a neck chain or thong.

Problems with Jump Rings?

1   The ring does not close properly leaving a gap - when you twisted the ring open you also pulled one end of the ring slightly to the side. Start again with a new ring - make sure that you keep your elbows down by your sides as you roll the pliers and just move your wrist. It sometimes helps to put your elbows on the table to give you a good firm base for your hands as they hold the pliers. If you are still getting a small gap twist the jump ring open a tiny amount - now twist the ring shut whilst pushing the pliers towards one another - this will squeeze the gap shut.

2   The ring does not close properly as the ends overlap - when you twisted the ring open and shut you also pushed the two ends of the ring together. Start again with a new ring - as above keep your elbows in or rest on the table top - practice just rolling your wrist away from you and back again - the ring will open easily. If it is difficult to bend you are using too much pressure and pushing the pliers too hard which will cause the ends to crossover.

3   The ring breaks opposite the opening - you have twisted the ring too far - just open it enough to drop in the components that you need to join together - the less you bend the ring the stronger it will be.

Jump Rings are Workbox Essentials

Make a beaded chain more flexible by using jump rings between all of the links

hen you bring
gether many
rands to make
tassel use a jump
g at the top of each
rand - if you omit the
mp rings the strands
n tend to stick out and
t fall softly into place.

Make a simple fan shaped tassel pendant with 0.8mm wire. Join the strands together on a jump ring and pull up through a top bead on an eyepin.

Use small jump rings to attach clasps to the back of necklaces and bracelets. Oval jump rings are especially useful on heavy designs.

Use jump rings to attach charms to heavyweight chain to make charm bracelets

Make a handbag charm from an assortment of beads, a bit of chain and lots of heavyweight jump rings

Use 6mm jump rings for strength on projects like this

There are three main considerations when choosing the correct threading method for your beads

1 The type of material and weight of your beads
2 The hole size in the beads
3 The design you want to make - short or long; multi-strand or floating style; bracelet or necklace (bracelets get a lot more wear and tear); soft and draping or extra strong and durable.

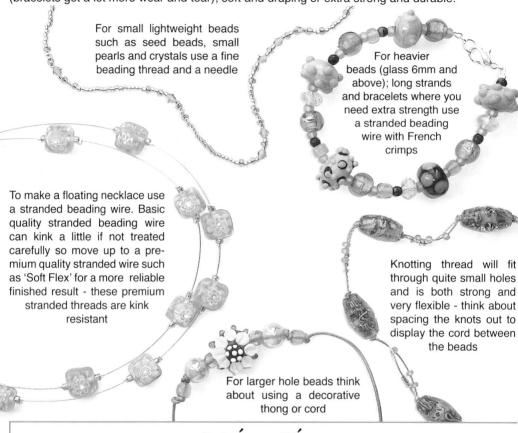

For small lightweight beads such as seed beads, small pearls and crystals use a fine beading thread and a needle

For heavier beads (glass 6mm and above); long strands and bracelets where you need extra strength use a stranded beading wire with French crimps

To make a floating necklace use a stranded beading wire. Basic quality stranded beading wire can kink a little if not treated carefully so move up to a premium quality stranded wire such as 'Soft Flex' for a more reliable finished result - these premium stranded threads are kink resistant

Knotting thread will fit through quite small holes and is both strong and very flexible - think about spacing the knots out to display the cord between the beads

For larger hole beads think about using a decorative thong or cord

Design Tips

1   Start with the central or feature beads of the design - lay them out in order.
2   Place smaller contrast beads in-between the larger feature beads to help the design to flex - small rounds and bicone shapes are great for this.
3   If you have lots of different colours and textures all together think about using one additional small bead style or colour to repeat down the length - this will bring the design together.
4   Check the hole sizes to make sure that the beads will not fall inside one another - if you have a wide variety of hole sizes think about using bead cups at either end of the largest holed beads to help them to centralise on the thread and not to swallow the smaller beads to either side.
5   Use smaller beads or seed beads to run out towards the clasp to make it comfortable to wear.
6   Always finish with a small bead next to the clasp - you will be able to use the clasp much more easily.

Stranded Beading Wire & French Crimps

Stranded beading wire is available in many colours and under many brand names but they all have the same basic structure. Multiple strands of very fine steel wire are twisted together to give strength and flexibility - this twisted rope is then covered in a thin film of plastic which can be dyed a multitude of colours. Premium stranded wires such as 'Soft Flex' have extra flexibility, kink resistance and can also have sterling silver or gold plated wire cores.

In general the finer the wires used down the centre of the plastic the more flexible the stranded wire will be and a higher number of wires will give you more strength. For most purposes a normal stranded beading wire with five to nine strands will be very suitable. Premium stranded wire will state both the thickness and number of the wires on the outside of the reel (up to 49 strands currently) together with an indication of the maximum load that the beading wire will take under normal usage.

French Crimps

Stranded wire is not finished with a knot but with a special crushable bead called a French crimp. Crimps are tiny beads or tubes made from a soft metal tape. They are available in different sizes (2mm tends to be the most useful).

To squash French crimps you will need to use a pair of flat faced pliers (chain nosed, flat nosed or snipe nosed) or a pair of crimping pliers.

Crimping pliers are specially shaped to crease and then fold the crimp as it closes down over the wire - it can look very neat if you practice a little first but you must use the correct size crimping pliers with the size of crimps you have chosen - flat pliers work with any size or shape of crimp.

Using Crimping Pliers

Before you use the crimping pliers on your finished work practice a little first - ten or so practice crimps will do the job. Thread a crimp onto a piece of beading wire and push your thumbnail up against it so that it sits square on the thread. Using the smile shaped hole (A) (see below) on the crimping pliers squeeze the crimp gently to put a crease into the crimp. Your thumbnail should keep the crimp square on the wire as you crimp - if the crimp twists it will not crease neatly.

Turn the crimp through 90° and place it in the round hole on the pliers (B). Push your nail up close to the crimp and gently squeeze down with the pliers so the crease becomes a fold.

The crimp will now be holding firmly onto the wire.

Crimping Pliers close-up

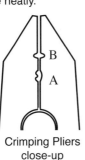

Using Flat Faced Pliers

Position the crimp just where you need it to be - if you are positioning the crimp along a blank length of thread push the crimp up against your thumbnail to hold it still.

Use the pliers close to the hinge end of the jaws - you get more control of the squeezing action there.

Squeeze down firmly but slowly - do not press down quickly or the crimp will twist and not grip into place. The crimp should go completely flat.

Finishing Off the End of Stranded Beading Wire

Cut a piece of stranded wire 15cm longer than you want your finished necklace or bracelet to be. Thread on your beads - if you are threading from one end you might like to use a piece of sticky tape on the other end of the wire to stop the beads from sliding off. Try to start and finish the design with a smallish bead (this makes it easier for you to work the clasp) and with a hole smaller than the French crimp that you need to use at the end (this makes it easier to use the crimp). Check that the design is long enough for your purposes - on average the clasp will add approximately 2cm to the finished length.

Thread a French crimp onto the end of the wire. Bend the end of the wire back towards the end of the design and pass it through the crimp to make a noose-like loop (fig 10).

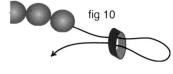

fig 10

Making sure that the beads are not falling off the other end of the design adjust the wire and the crimp to bring the loop size down to approximately 3mm in diameter. Using your flat pliers or crimping pliers secure the crimp (fig 11). If necessary trim the excess tigertail down to 2 - 3cm and bring up the last few beads of the design to hide the tail.

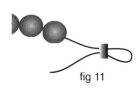

fig 11

Return to the other end of the wire - remove any sticky tape and thread on a French crimp. As before bend the wire into a loop passing it back through the crimp and the first few beads of the sequence (fig 12).

fig 12

Adjust the size of the loop to bring it down to match that at the other end of the design - DO NOT SQUASH THE CRIMP FLAT YET. As the wire will not stretch make sure that you have left enough 'give' in the length so that the necklace or bracelet will come around into a flexible circle to fit around your neck or wrist. Readjust the loop if necessary and secure the crimp. You will have a tail of wire sticking out from between the beads - trim it very carefully as closely as you can.

Attach your clasp with a jump ring to each end of the design.

A chunky bracelet finished with French crimps

Attach your clasp with jump rings

Making a Single Row Floating Necklace

Floating necklaces are easy and quick to make - the trick is to choose beads that have holes no bigger than your crimps and are approximately the same weight as one another - this type of design does not work well with a heavy centre bead - if you want to make a spaced design with a heavy centre bead or pendant see the instructions for decorative knots. Basic quality stranded beading wire can kink - if you are making a more complex design or using extra special beads make sure you pick a premium brand wire.

You Will Need

50cm of stranded wire thread
Beads to decorate the wire (minimum of five / maximum of ten)
Two crimps for each of the decorative beads chosen plus four crimps for the ends
Two small beads for the ends of the design (approximately 4mm in diameter is ideal)
A clasp set with jump rings to attach

Plan out your design on a surface in front of you. Make sure you have your small end beads at either end ready to conceal the thread ends. Thread onto the first end one crimp, one of your end beads and one crimp (fig 13). Fold the end of the wire over and pass through the end crimp and into the bead (not out the other side of the bead) fig 14. Pull on the long free end of the wire to pull the loop down to size and squash the crimps to secure (fig 15).

Thread on the decorative beads with one crimp on either side of each bead (fig 16) make sure that the holes in the beads do not swamp the crimps - if necessary use a seed bead or similar either side of each bead to prevent the crimps from falling inside the bigger beads.

DO NOT SQUEEZE THE CRIMPS YET

fig 13   fig 14   fig 15

fig 16

At the far end thread on one crimp. Measure the design and position the new crimp 1cm short of the final finished length. Squeeze the crimp into place. Thread on the second end bead and the final crimp. Bend the end of the wire over and pass back through the end crimp and the 4mm bead (fig 17). Pull on the wire end to reduce the loop down to size and squeeze the end crimp. Trim the wire carefully and add the clasp.

With the length of the necklace set you can now see the position of the centre front of the necklace and can more easily space out the beads into the correct places for your design. Arrange the beads with a crimp pushed up close to either side of each bead. When you are happy with the design squeeze the crimps into place.

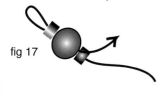

fig 17

Designing with Stranded Beading Wire & Crimps

Curls and Flounces

Stranded wire threads will curl into fantastic bouncy swirls and tendrils. Run your thumbnail along the wire to the end - you cannot control the direction of the curls but more pressure with your nail makes the wire more curly so take it slowly and apply a tiny bit of pressure first - increase the pressure until you have the effect you want. Then bead the wire at intervals using crimps as stoppers.

fig 18

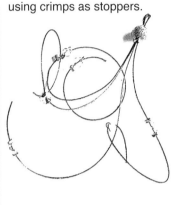

Multi Row Floating Necklaces

A 2mm French crimp will take up to three lengths of flexible beading wire but you need a little technique to make it look neat.

1 Hold all three wires together and thread on a crimp, a small bead and a crimp.

2 Fold one of the wire ends over and push into the end crimp to make a loop. Withdraw the other two wires so they are concealed inside the bead (fig 18). Squash the crimps flat to secure the arrangement.

3 Now thread on your decorative beads with the extra crimps required to space out the design - do not squash these crimps yet.

4 Finish off the far side of the necklace as above using a small bead to conceal the cut ends.

5 Complete the design by spacing out the decorative beads with the crimps. Add the clasp with jump rings.

Stranded Wire Earrings

One length of wire is folded in half to make the top loop. Both ends pass down through a crimp, a bead and a crimp.

Before the crimps are secured a third length of wire is pushed up into the bottom crimp (fig 19) - this gives you three ends to decorate.

fig 19

Stranded Wire Hoops

Use a larger crimp bead or tube and one length of wire to make a figure of eight (or a double figure of eight for the double hoops below). The ends of the wire need to crossover inside the crimp (fig 20). Squash the crimp flat and trim off the ends neatly.

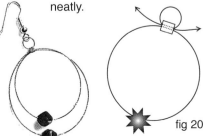

fig 20

Using Fine Beading Thread with a Needle

Beading thread is used for small lightweight beads and woven designs. You can straight-string 6mm beads on beading thread providing that the overall length does not exceed 60cm. If you want to make a longer necklace with 6mm beads and larger sized beads use stranded beading wire instead. Beading thread is usually made from stranded nylon, it has several trade names - Nymo, Superlon, KO etc. The threads are available in different thicknesses - D is the most common; A is a little finer and AA finer still.

Beading Needles

These special needles have finer eyes than normal sewing needles. 'Size 10 Beading' will do most things although you might need a thinner 'Size 13 Beading' for very tiny beads. For straight stringing fine beads such as freshwater pearls try a twisted wire needle which has a collapsible eye for easy threading.

Using Beading Thread

In general if you are straight stringing a design it is best to use a double thickness of thread on your beading needle. For woven designs a single thickness is better as it tends not to tangle so much. Whichever design you make you will need to finish off the threads ends.

You can either

make a concealed knot to hide the thread ends

or

add a clasp using calotte ends to hold the knots firmly

The threads come together through the feature beads and the occasional seed bead to keep the strands in line and the design secure.

A double thickness of beading thread is used for each of the strands you see here. The needle passes down the pendant, through a stopper bead at the bottom and back up to the top of the pendant. The design is finished with calotte crimps.

If you want a simple fine bead bracelet without a clasp think about using transparent elastic thread instead. You don't need a needle but to make it easy to thread through the beads put a tiny dab of plain talc on the end of the thread. Tie the ends together and dab with a little clear nail polish When the knot is dry trim the ends closely.

Using Calotte Crimps

Have a close look at a calotte (fig 21) - you will see two cups hinged together with a hook at one end. Having a closer look at the hinge you will see a hole - this is where the thread ends run into the calotte. The knot will sit in one of the cups and the other cup will close down to conceal it. The hook will attach permanently to one end of the clasp set. If you compare the size of the hole for the thread and the diameter of the thread you will see that you will need to make a very large knot to hold the thread ends inside the cup - to avoid the difficulty of this we will use a very small seed bead to make knot a little larger.

fig 21

Attaching Calottes to Double Thickness Beading Thread

Thread the needle and bring the two cut ends of the thread together. Onto one end of the thread only, pass one of the smallest seed beads that you have and push it down towards the needle. Hold the two ends of the thread together and make a simple knot (fig 22). This traps the bead on the thread.

fig 22

Pass the needle from the inside to the outside of the calotte through the thread hole to bring the bead to sit inside the calotte cups (fig 23). Thread on sufficient beads to make your necklace or bracelet (the clasp will add 2cm to the finished length).

fig 23

fig 24

fig 25

Pass the needle through the hole on a second calotte to emerge on the inside of the cups. Make sure there are no gaps between the beads along the design.

Cut the needle off the thread leaving two long tails. Thread a single tiny seed bead onto one side of the thread and push down into the open cup (fig 24). Tie the two thread ends together (fig 25) to push the bead into the cup. Repeat the knot to secure.

Dab the knots with a little clear nail polish or glue and leave to dry. Use the tails of the thread to help you to position the small single beads in the middle of the cups as you close the calottes. Trim the excess thread away with the tips of your scissors. Hook the calottes over the end of the clasp set and close down with a pair of pliers.

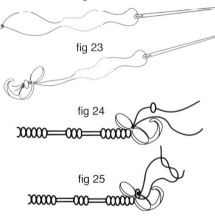

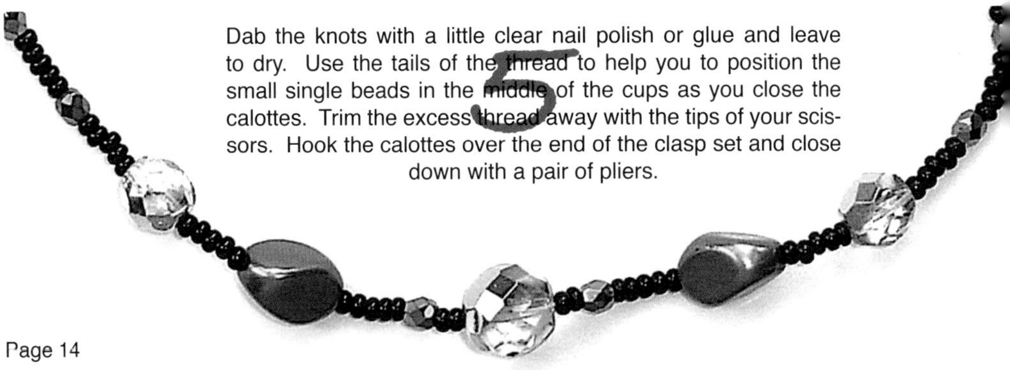

Making a Double or Triple Row Design with Calottes

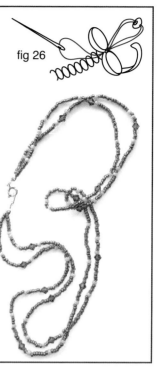

fig 26

Start the project as for a single row design but make sure you have enough thread length to make the extra row. When you pass the needle into the calotte at the far end of the design do not cut off the needle. Thread on a small seed bead and pass the needle back through the hole in the calotte to emerge alongside the last bead of the design (fig 26) - this will pull the seed bead up into an anchor inside the calotte. You can now start the second row.

Once you have threaded the second row pass the needle through to the inside of the first calotte.

If you want to add a third row pass the needle through the seed bead inside the calotte and out through the hole in the calotte to start the next row.

If you want to finish off the thread cut the thread to one side of the needle only giving you a loose end and the other end still threaded on the needle. Pass the needle through the seed bead inside the calotte. You can now tie the two ends of the thread together in a simple knot to secure. Dab the knots to seal with clear nail polish or similar and close the calottes.

Making a Concealed Knot

If you make a necklace that is long enough to pop over the head you do not need to add a clasp - you can simply tie the beads into a continuous loop. However you will need to do this correctly to get a professional finish. Tie the two ends of the beading together with a double knot (fig 27).

fig 27

fig 28

fig 29

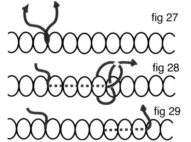

Pass the needle end of the thread back along the 4 - 6 beads to one side of the knot and make a knot around the thread between the beads there. Repeat the knot (fig 28).

Pass through a few more beads before trimming (fig 29). Return to the other thread end(s) and re-attach the needle. Repeat in the other direction to neaten off these ends as well. Seal all the knots with a dab of nail polish to secure.

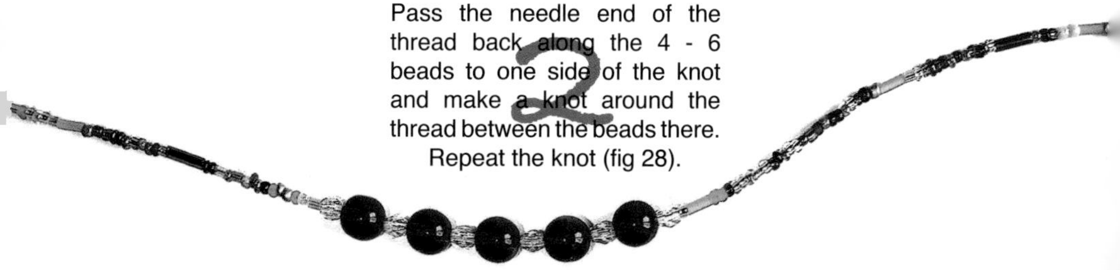

Simple Decorative Ideas with Needle & Thread

Making Daisies

Daisies are quick and easy motifs to add to your design - pick colours of seed beads in the same size - one for the petals and one for the centre. You will need a third seed bead (same size or smaller) for the stringing that shows in-between the daisies You will need a bit more thread than for a straight string of beads.

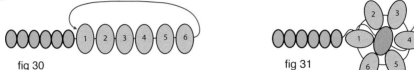

fig 30

fig 31

Thread on a few of your stringing seed beads before you make the flower. Now thread on six petal beads. Pass the needle through the first of the six beads again in the same direction as it was originally threaded (fig 30). This will bring the six beads into a circle. If necessary adjust the tension in the thread so the circle is up tight to the first few beads of the sequence. Thread on the seed bead for the centre of the flower. Count around to the fourth seed bead petal and pass the needle through this bead in the opposite direction than it was originally threaded (fig 31) to draw the centre bead into the middle of the flower. Thread on a few spacing beads before you start the next flower.

Make a Fringe Strand

fig 32

fig 33

Thread on the beads you want for your fringe strand. Thread on one extra bead to anchor the strand (yellow bead in fig 32). Leaving aside the anchor bead pass the needle back up the other beads of the fringe strand. Before you continue the stringing pass the needle through the last bead of the stringing above the fringe strand to central-ise the strand below this bead - note the direction of the thread through the bead. The fringe strand will then hang properly (fig 33).

Multi-Branched
Coral Style Fringing

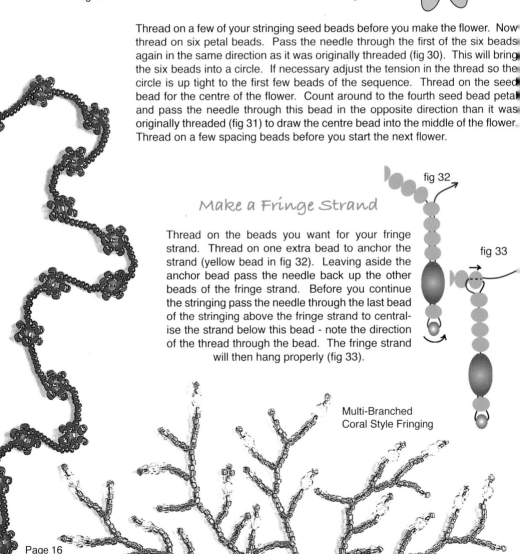

Thonging, Cords & Sliding Knots

The term thonging refers to any thicker thread that can be decorated with beads. Thonging is usually made from cotton or leather, although it is now also available as a manmade microfibre suede and in lots of fancy finish cords like rattail, which is used for decorative Chinese-style knotting; coloured and metallic elastics; coloured hemp and C-Lon macrame threads. They are all available in different diameters for different sorts of beads and different types of design.

Using Thonging with Beads

Because thonging and beading cords are thicker than the standard beading threads you will need to use beads with a larger hole. Some beads will only fit onto finer thongs - some will take thicker thongs or more than one strand of the finer sizes. Some beads are deceptively difficult to thread onto a thong - hollow beads where it is difficult to find the hole at the other side of the bead and beads with roughened holes which snag the thonging. When your beads are threaded you will need to add a fastener - you can finish the cord with either spiral or box shaped lace ends or make a sliding knot for an adjustable fit.

Threading Your Beads

Because the end of the thong can fray as you are threading it is best to plan out your design before you start.

Bring together your selection for the design and try out different sequences on a flat surface in front of you. If you have a lot of beads to thread harden the end of the thong first in a little nail polish When the varnish is dry, cut the hardened end into a point and begin to thread - it should now fit through many beads before it starts to fray.

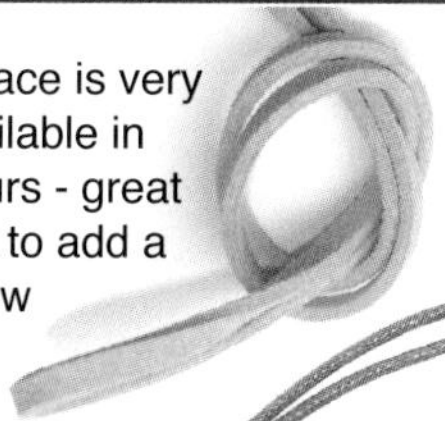

Microfibre flat lace is very strong and available in gorgeous colours - great if you just want to add a pendant or a few simple beads

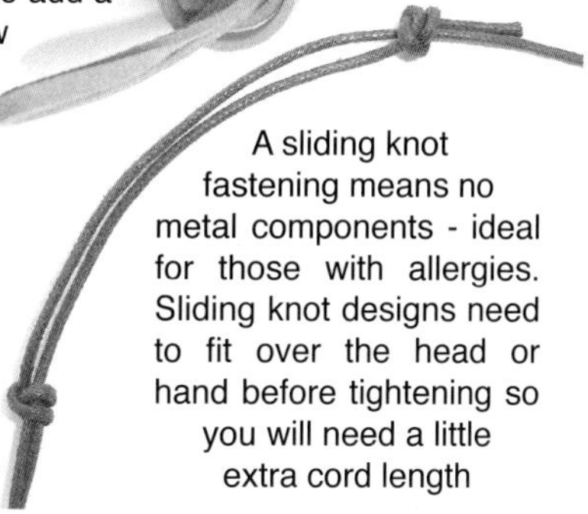

Cotton cord is available in three diameters - 0.5mm, 1.0mm and 2.0mm - the end can fray a bit as you thread on the beads - see above

Rattail is silky and makes beautiful decorative knots

A sliding knot fastening means no metal components - ideal for those with allergies. Sliding knot designs need to fit over the head or hand before tightening so you will need a little extra cord length

Sliding Knots for Thonging and Cords

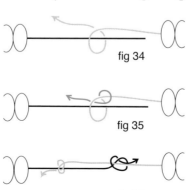

A sliding knot can be used instead of a clasp but you need to have at least 80cm of cord for a necklace as it fits over the head before tightening. Thread up the design and tie a knot at each end of the design to keep the beads in the centre. Cross the cords over at the back so that they lie parallel to one another. Pick up the first end and wrap it once around the cord from the other side (fig 34).

fig 34

fig 35

fig 36

Bring the cord back over the top of the loop just made and pass it through the loop (fig 35) to make a knot.
Repeat with the other end of the thong to make two knots pointing in opposite directions (fig 36). Pull the knots down towards the beads and the necklace shortens - push the knots together and the necklace is long enough to fit over the head.

Lace Ends

Spiral Lace Ends are designed to use with a thick round thong however the diagrams show that if you fold over the last 8mm of a thinner thong before you push it into the lace end the spiral lace end will work very well for a thinner thong too.

Push the thong end into the socket end of the lace end - if you are using a thinner thong fold the end over a little so you get a snug fit (fig 37). Rotate the lace end in your fingers until you locate the end of the spring at the socket end . Place your flat pliers onto the socket end of the lace end so you just catch the very end of the spring with the top jaw and the underside of the spring with the lower jaw.

fig 37

fig 38

Gently squeeze down - this will fold the last quarter turn of the lace end down onto the lace to secure (fig 38).

Repeat at the far end of the design.

Finished with box ends this design uses three strands of C-Lon macrame thread in a a simple woven lattice pattern

These wooden beads have large holes so a thicker thong and spiral ends are used for a secure finish

A thin thong is needed to fit through the glass beads in this design so box lace ends were chosen to make a neat finish

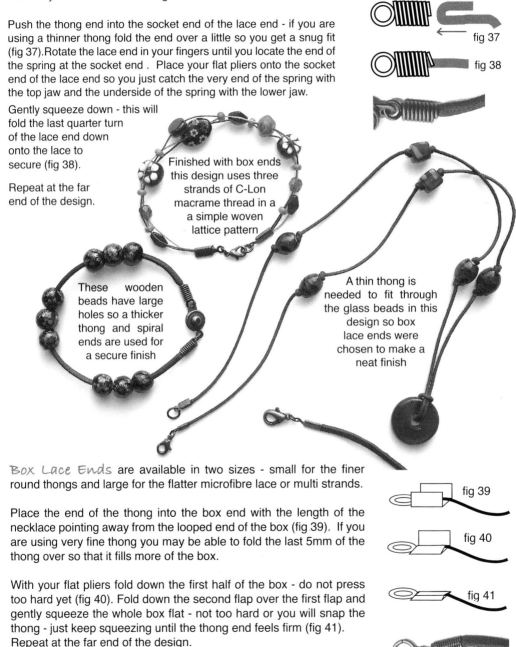

Box Lace Ends are available in two sizes - small for the finer round thongs and large for the flatter microfibre lace or multi strands.

Place the end of the thong into the box end with the length of the necklace pointing away from the looped end of the box (fig 39). If you are using very fine thong you may be able to fold the last 5mm of the thong over so that it fills more of the box.

fig 39

fig 40

With your flat pliers fold down the first half of the box - do not press too hard yet (fig 40). Fold down the second flap over the first flap and gently squeeze the whole box flat - not too hard or you will snap the thong - just keep squeezing until the thong end feels firm (fig 41). Repeat at the far end of the design.

fig 41